SECOND LI

By

Karl Tearney

First published 2019 by Fly on the Wall Poetry Press

Published in the UK by
Fly on the Wall Poetry Press
56 High Lea Rd
New Mills
Derbyshire
SK22 3DP

www.flyonthewallpoetry.co.uk

ISBN 978-1-9995986-6-2

978-1-9995986-6-2

A CIP Catalogue record for this book is available from the British Library.

"My view of the world has changed so much these past four years and whilst life continues its ups and downs the one constant is how incredibly lucky I am to have words."

Dedicated to Wayne 1966 – 1977

I would like to thank Emma for all of her encouragement, Kristal for her kind support, all of my friends and family and even my former lovers. None of this would have been achievable without you all. I would also like to mention how incredibly supportive all of you that have read my work and commented have been. You've been fundamental in bringing about this book. Lastly, I would like to thank Isabelle for having the faith in my work and publishing it for me.

"I heard Karl perform his poetry for the first time at a Style for Soldiers dinner, in support of injured veterans. Far from being a lover of poetry, Karl's brilliant emotive poems had everyone and myself in the room transfixed on him and his words. I think I have been his number 1 fan ever since. When Brietling asked me to direct their WW1 centenary commemorations Film for the RAF, I knew there was only one man that could capture the emotion that could capture the poignancy as well as the romance of the RAF within a few short words.

A room full of at first reluctant executives were stunned, most with goose bumps, some almost in tears when I read out Karl's Poem for the first time.
His numerous poetic expressions of the impact of post traumatic stress disorder following his time as a pilot in the British Forces for over 35 years are a testimony to the passion, courage and selflessness of our servicemen and women.
Through Karl's poetry they and the sacrifices made will never be forgotten."

- David James Gandy

"Karl Tearney writes from the heart and the gut, and he has both in abundance. Do read this, and feel humbled"

- Charles Dance

"Karl's poems have flowed into my inbox for our a year now since he sent me a beautiful thank you verse for a party my charity 'Style for Soldiers' had given; 'I used to be Soldier, I marched along with pride…' I wept as I read this moving, powerful and deeply thoughtful poem and shortly after made contact with Karl, discovering how poetry was his fundamental medication that no other therapy had helped. We have since worked together, encouraging other veterans to write and perform poetry and Karl has brought joy and inspiration to many children with poetry workshops in schools, as well as attracting the British press and media to feature he and his work. He is an exceptional man, writing poetry that is accessible to all, voicing the struggles as well as the beauty of our times and affirming to anyone the psychological healing powers of creativity."

- Emma Willis MBE

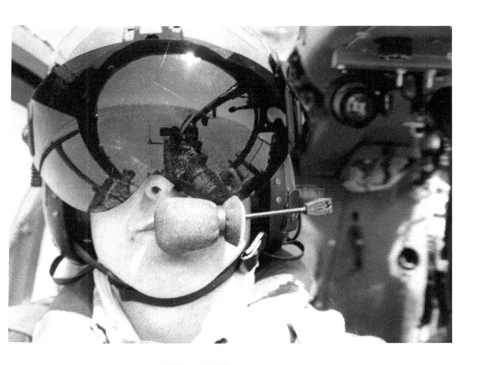

Karl Tearney:

My Mental Mind

So I joined the British Army as a boy soldier in the early summer of 1983, after spending a short spell in horological design. I had always wanted to be a pilot and sadly had missed out large periods of schooling because of a few issues with my parent's divorce and my moving from parent to parent.

I had joined the Army Air Corps and had to serve firstly on the ground before any application was allowed to apply for a flying role. It was late in 1990 that I attended the Aircrew section centre, which at that time, was in RAF Biggin Hill. I was so pleased when I passed and could then complete the remainder of the Army selection process before beginning my pilot's course in 1992.

Upon completion of my course in 1993, I was chosen to then go straight to Operational flying in Northern Ireland. I had a tough 26 months and witnessed the harsh reality of terrorism seldom seen on the news. It's odd how when serving on the ground, you become fixated on your patch of ground and rarely think of anyone elsewhere. When in the air, your responsibility becomes much greater.

Much of my time was spent hopping from incident to incident and I rarely had the time to ponder on events, as the pressure was so high. I remember getting very little sleep whilst there, as my mind was awash with imagery and thought. No one spoke of any of the incidents after, apart from a few quick debriefs at the end of the duty. The macho image of being a soldier, entwined with the expectancy of being completely lucid because you are a pilot seemed nonsense to me - but that was how we lived.

Just 5 months or so after Northern Ireland, I deployed to Bosnia as part of the implementation force (IFOR) and I had neither idea nor preparation for what was in store. Everything was a mess, buildings, roads, power, water, and people were all in tatters. The things I witnessed still haunt me today and especially those involving children.

Upon my return, I knew there was something wrong in my head and I sought help. The Army counseling team seemed unusually interested in my own childhood rather than my recollections of Northern Ireland and then Bosnia. I found that very frustrating and thankfully returned to work.

Various things (that one might say are just part of life) then happened over the next decade or so and I remained in the Army until, quite suddenly, I began to sob uncontrollably at night. I had no idea as to why but oddly I didn't tire from not being able to sleep. It carried on nightly for a month, until one morning my work phone rang and I couldn't talk. I simply began to cry and couldn't stop. That was my last day at work, as I then spent time in recovery including a spell as an inpatient in a mental health hospital.

Since then, I have struggled to get better. I tried all sorts of therapy, but each time it resulted in my feeling worse and being discharged as 'treatment intolerant'. My problem is that I don't have a single point of trauma. I have 3000 flying hours of trauma, stemming from many operational areas.

I concluded I would have to find a way to treat myself and turned to writing. I went for a short walk and wrote about a willow tree that was nearby. The words flowed into a poem, my first ever, and I've written almost every day since.

What has been remarkable about my story is that I realised I will never find the old me but the new one has a remarkable gift, poetry. I have now had some success including work at RADA, the Hay Literature Festival, promotion of poetry as therapy on the BBC News and the recently released a RAF Centenary poem.

My work now spans all subjects and I have released a children's poetry book through the *Style For Soldier's* Charity, which was donated to all the children of the injured service people, on the charity's books. I have also spent time at the second largest special needs school, The Milestone School, Gloucester, teaching them about how the use of art and words can be fundamental to finding inner peace, when struggling inside a torn mind.

Contents

My Mental Mind

Love

Moments

My Mental Mind

The void

In the centre of the universe
There stands a lonely man
He used to live on planet earth
But now, no longer can

Surrounded by a thousand suns
They brighten up his face
But hidden deep beneath his skin
The charcoaled dark of space

We all have sunlight in our life
The darkness comes and goes
Not it seems for lonely man
Whose troubles no one knows

The Dark Wood

I'm in the wood, the darkened wood
I know not why I'm here
I can sense the warmth of sunshine air
As the sun tries to appear

I can hear the voices, they are so loud
I can't tell what they say
There are calming words amidst the din
They sound so far away

The mist so thick, upon the ground
It hides the thick decay
Things are moving around my feet
Could this be my doomsday?

My body sore, in so much pain
I'm struggling for breath
The air in here just seems so thin
This place just smells of death

I'd like to talk, to talk to you
I just can't find the words
Its whilst I'm searching in my head
This wood fills with blackbirds

You shouldn't come, come to this place
You must stand in the sun
Because one day I'll find a way:
A way to you I'll run

The things you never see

I stand before the butcher
His apron masked in blood
I withdraw into memories
The cleaver makes a thud

Metal breaks beneath my skin
Then wolves patrol my brain
Punches landing everywhere
The pain I can't contain

Sweet misery on misery
The butcher strikes once more
Skin and muscle ripped apart
My remnants hit the floor

Rivers flowing through my eyes
Bullets piercing ears
Blood erupting everywhere
A sum of all my fears

Sweet misery on misery
The butcher strikes again
Skin and muscle ripped apart
My body shakes in pain

Locust feast inside of me
My heartbeats start to slow
Voices come from everywhere
This sorrow all I know.

My Mask

I wear a mask that looks like me:
Try to look but you won't see

Behind that mask I hide my fears
Inside the mask I hide my tears

Fading

So far away the faintest light
Perhaps a distant star
The only light that I can see
It's dim glow from afar

I shout and scream then cry to God
Darkening regardless
Spurned, ignored and cast aside
No healer of my darkness

Underground

I'm lost in my own underground
The signs have all long gone
I wander round the corridors
Those journeys always wrong

I hear the trains come rattling by
They never ever stop
I climb and climb so many steps
Yet never reach the top

Sometimes I meet a plague of rats
They snarl and hiss at me
I turn around and run away
They laugh at what they see

Other days the lights go out
I grope around the dark
Hands touch things that frighten me
My terror now so stark

There are some days I see a train
I see you all on board
I wave at you and shout hello
My screams for help ignored

So next time that you're on the tube
And see that platform bare
Take some time to look for me
As you might see me there

Today and every day

Non-stop lightning bolts
Are striking in my brain
Thunderclaps are echoing
The noise is just insane

Non-stop stabbing pains
Are striking in my heart
Blood is shrieking everywhere
Electric shocks now start

Non-stop tidal waves
Are building in my eyes
Their force is just unstoppable
A tsunami sweeping cries

Non-stop hurricanes
Are stealing all my breath
The lack of air is killing me
Vacuums threaten death

Non-stop shards of glass
Are coursing through my skin
Tearing all in front of them
They travel from within

Non-stop becomes unstoppable
These things are every day
The mental torture evidence
The pain from yesterday

Thunder heart

I can hear the thunder grumble
Yet still no sign of rain
I can see the brightest flashes
My heaven seems in pain

Bright stars are falling in my heart
Their fall like magic rain
A thousand tiny butterflies
Now dance as if insane

I can hear the thunder grumble
Electric shocks my brain
I can see the brightest flashes
This heaven hurts again

The stars now dimming from my view
No magic left to see
No butterflies to flap their wings
My heart sinks to the sea

I can hear the thunder grumble
Coming faster than a train
I can see the brightest flashes
And now here comes the rain

Reflecting

Reflecting on the tiny pond
The sun, the sky, the tree
But I am not reflected there
There is no sign of me

Reflecting on my yesterdays
Bright colours kept me free
That was long before my death
My ghost now all you see

Reflecting on what could have been
Perhaps my birth the key
Not wanted as a little boy
My parent's pond a sea

Doctor Who?

My eyes just cannot X-ray
Nor can they MRI
I cannot see your blood cells
So why, I ask oh why
Can people judge my trauma?
Then question how I feel
Suggesting I'm not poorly
Or tell me how to heal
So many bloody experts
None of whom will know
Exactly how I'm feeling
But still say so and so

Now please I ask you just one thing
Take off your doctor's coat
Accept that you're not qualified
Not qualified to gloat

End of days

My afternoon is ending
Sunset brings its fear
My devils only come at night
Chasing me
Haunting me
Taunting me
Hating me
Killing me
Thrilling me
Consuming me
Only sunrise sets me free
Come sunrise set me free

Because

I cried a thousand tears today
I cried for what I was
The thoughts of who I should have been
For what I was because
Those cherished thoughts of what I was
The motionless of time
For I am simply who I am
The man that lives because
The terrors left by yesterday
They fill my head with hurt
I'm left to battle them alone
Because I am because

Landslide

The tragedies that mark our lives
Can bring us so much pain
Another time, another place
We'd dance in sun-drenched rain

My walls of stone are very firm
But not the clay beneath
Sometimes the sinking will not stop
Great bricks slide underneath

And as the years go fleeting by
We await the warming sun
To stop the wall from sliding down
Then shore up what we've done

But in those times of great decay
We return to what we know
To fight the wind and rain that falls
Then hope for sun or snow

My Theatre

The curtain closes once again
This show just can't go on
Tiredness is strangling
The spotlights now long gone

The theatre is quiet now
The scenery knocked down
All around just empty seats
They wear a dusty brown

Nothing moving in the dark
Bright lights now ashen grey
No second glances anymore
The crowds now stay away

The air is heavy, yet so still
You won't see much in there
The atmosphere has lost its life
My ghosts now everywhere

There is

There is beauty in sadness
There is dark amongst light
There is death amongst living
There are losers that fight

There is time for the thinkers
There is time for the brave
There's no time for the takers
As they march to the grave

But mixed up in this madness
There are things we don't see
An emotional landscape
Come now, see it with me

There is pain amidst passion
There is loss amongst love
There is joy after crying
There's below up above

There is selfish and selfless
There is pleasure in pain
There's a heart for the heartless
And a rainbow in rain

But mixed up in this madness
There are things we don't see
An emotional landscape
Come now, see it with me

There's a start to an ending
There are words about words
There is hate amongst friendship
There's six ninths or two thirds

There is sense in the senseless
There's a me next to you
There are two ways to see things
Now I hope you see too

Steam

Your brain is like a steam engine
With a tender full of coal
It flies along the flattest lines
The coal burn takes no toll

But sometimes there's a hill to climb
The engine starts to slow
You need more coal to help it out
Your fuel stock now runs low

You cannot help the other trains
As they journey up the hill
You just don't have the coal on board
And there's nowhere to refill

So please I say, take care on board
Then journey where you can
That coal won't last forevermore
Remember you're one man

Learn from me

Darkened vacuums fill my soul
My blood now rusty red
My heart so full of loneliness
Inside my head is dead

I write these words in solitude
Sat by my willow tree
The place where I record my life
To escape in poetry

I hope that one day, when I'm gone
My soul will shine for you
To help you reach into your soul
Then focus on your view

For life should be so beautiful
Not one of endless pain
So reach out for your happiness
Then dance amidst the rain

The tiny door

In the deepest recess of your mind
There lies a tiny door
It's bolted closed and locked up tight
A door you should ignore

Through happy days and joyous times
The door stays out of sight
But if you're ever struck by stress
That door is lit with light

Depression holds the key quite tight
The door now opens wide
Tainted calls will suck you in
Beware of what's inside

Ghostly spirits, good and bad
Will dance around the room
You simplify the things you see
From present to the womb

That's when that room gets very dark
So dark that you can't see
The noise and touches everywhere
Your brain's own purgatory

Outside you look the very same
No one can see the pain
The tiny door now locks you in
Condemned inside your brain

I'm so sorry

I haven't been myself of late
I've struggled deep inside
There's something that I need to say
Und so es tut mir leid!

My hand is reaching out to you
So too my inner soul
My mental health is stopping me
Et donc je suis désolé

We all speak many dialects
Some people come and go
So please don't leave me all alone
Y así que lo siento

Banshee

Empty
I feel empty
Just bones wrapped in tardy flesh
Pointless
I feel pointless
There's nothing here to thresh

Empty
I feel empty
Nothing lives beneath my skin
Pointless
I feel pointless
No real feelings live within

Empty
I feel empty
Coldness of winter within
Pointless
I feel pointless
No summer sun to break in

Empty
I feel empty
There is nothing here but me
Pointless
I feel pointless
I await my own bashee

Ozone hole

A chalice full of poison
Is placed inside of me
So when you're in my company
That poison will leak free

A pocketful of darkness
Sits just below my skin
So when you're in my company
Your darkness will begin

A head so full of sadness
Is fighting to break free
So when you're in my company
You'll feel your misery

A heart that's barely beating
My blood so barely warm
So when you're in my company
Be ready for my storm

Sullen words lay in my throat
No room for words of joy
So when you're in my company
You'll see the word, destroy

Inside my chest hides jealousy
It wants to be like you
So when you're in my company
Be mindful what you do

The rest of me is poetry
My way into your soul

So when you're in my company
Let's shrink the ozone hole

Black dog

Please don't talk of a black dog
He doesn't follow me
For I've a flock of demons
That you will never see
So please just send me Angels
To come and set me free
They needn't come from heaven
But will need empathy

David

I feel like I am David
With slingshot and small stones
I fight Goliath daily
I fight his moans and groans

With stones so small and very round
I strike toward his head
He stumbles, then falls to his knees
He looks at me with dread

There are some days I have no stones
Nothing to battle him
He crushes me with all his might
Then taunts me at his whim

So on those days of victory
Proud David you will see
But on those days I have no stones
You'll see the ghost of me

Dirty cotton wool

Swathes of dirty cotton wool
Are filling up my sky
They roll and break quite violently
As they come tumbling by

There is no sign of sun nor moon
No shelter here for me
But still the sky looks eloquent
Its beauty there to see

I sit and watch that sullen sky
Then wait until the rain
For it will wash away the drought
So life can start again

A poem with no life

A thought has just come over me
I realised I'm not here
A deathly ghost, I roam this earth
Now lifeless in my fear

Post-Traumatic Stress Disorder

Post-Traumatic Stress Disorder
Such a stupid name
It's just a silly acronym
That means I am insane

Post-Traumatic Stress Disorder
What does that mean to me
Solitude, fear, anxiety
I'm not who I should be

Post-Traumatic Stress Disorder
You've simply no idea
I spend my time just wandering
My life consumed with fear

Post-Traumatic Stress Disorder
I'm trapped inside a cell
Taunted by the devil's men
They make my life such hell

Post-Traumatic Stress Disorder
I wish you'd set me free
But sadly that's not possible
You've got a grip on me

Post-Traumatic Stress Disorder
You take up all my time
You soak up all my happiness
Discard it like a crime

Post-Traumatic Stress Disorder
I don't mean to be blunt
You just can't see this thing you do
You're such a bloody ....

My House

You pass my door
Assume I'm out
But why not stop
And look about

For on the outside
The house looks strong
Yet on the inside
Something's wrong

Firm brick walls
No longer there
The floorboards creak
There is no stair

So bring a hammer
A chisel too
To help me mend
To help renew

As without help
This house won't stay
For it will crumble
Just fall away

So please my friends
I beg of you
Knock on my door
And help me through.

The Plane

The left wing falls
Perhaps the right
I'm falling fast
The harness tight
Controls are shaking
Violently
I cannot stop
I can't break free

Round and Round
And round I go
I try to stop
I cannot slow
Ground is coming
Oh so fast
Not sure how long
This flight can last

My brain's the pilot
And me the plane
To me it's simple
To you insane
I can't control
What I can't see
This planes not real
Just fantasy

Sinking

The waters cold
And murky too
Waves are crashing
I can't see you

I've fought so hard
To stay up here
But now I'm tired
Of all this fear

It's just too easy
To sink down deep
To reach the calm
No place to weep

I've drowned before
The panic short
A lifetime film
Your last report

Then emptiness
And fade away
Your troubles gone
That final day

Fog

The fog is back
It's really dense
I squint my eyes
I'm feeling tense

Nothing there
Nothing here
I'm all alone
Now trapped in fear

There is no forward
Nor any back
No up, nor down
No beaten track

I cannot find
Which way to go
Nor where I've been
I just don't know

This fog's not real
You just can't see
I'm deep inside
My memory

A Leaf

I'm a leaf without much colour
I look as if see-through
My contours start to dissipate
I'm not sure what to do

I'm in a world of colour
The vibrancy quite vast
The flash of colours everywhere
But mine have faded fast

I cover myself with paper
Use sticky bits of glue
Make myself look colourful
It makes me look like you

But bits 'n' bobs will never last
They crumble, fall like dust
I've tried that option many times
To all my friends' disgust

So what I need is nurturing
A nice safe place to stay
A place that I find comfortable
So I don't fade away

Then I can grow my leaf again
To make it nice and strong
Give it a tint, a subtle hue
So then I will belong

It won't be quick nor easy
It's going to take some time
With all of you supporting me
My leaf will be sublime

Ending

Saturated
Unloved
Insecure
Confused
Ineffable
Distressed
Emotional

Love

Wanted

Eyes that are sparkling
The soft plumping cheeks
The arrival of dimples
A mouth edge that creeks

My need for a smile
To say we're ok
To signal you like me
To brighten my day

I long for such beauty
I need it so much
I
So
Want
To
Feel
Your
Kindness
And
Touch

Yesterday today

I spent a moment yesterday
Inside my broken heart
Searching for the answers there
I know it wasn't smart
My heart is full of agony
The battle scars immense
The ghosts of people said to care
Their passion now past tense
The first aid teams now hard at work
To help me start anew
For I have faith that someone kind
Will see things as I do
Today is not the day before
I like the way I am
Always holding onto hope
A simple caring man

Unknowing

Is all that we are?
Is all that we were?
My life
My love
A litterateur

How can we move on?
When nobody listens?
My life
My love
My lonely light glistens

Seductress

She whispered softly in my ear
Excitement took control
I listened to her every word
As each one struck my soul

She looked at me with sexy eyes
Ran fingers through her hair
She giggled so excitedly
I couldn't help but stare

Her short blue dress was perfect
And so her heels too
I want to touch her silken skin
I think she wants that too

She moved to stand in front of me
She filled my heart with fire
Her arm outstretched toward my face
I was drenched in her desire

She ran her finger down my face
But lingered on my lips
Her body lowered gracefully
She slowly moved her hips

I was now frozen to my chair
She had complete control
She moistened lips whilst leaning in
I sensed what was her goal

I closed my eyes and wanted her
I felt her lips touch mine
A thousand volts shook over me
They travelled down my spine

She then sat down upon my knee
Like the cat that got the cream
I think that I was mesmerized
Or was this just a dream

Crash

I see the crash is coming
As I head toward the wall
Time stands still for just a while
As I shrink into a ball

Fighting you
Fighting me
Fighting things
I cannot see

Then there is the aftershock
My body seems stuck still
My mind is full of nothing now
Yet you look set to kill

Fighting you
Fighting me
Fighting things
You cannot see

Still confused and unsure why
I'm slipping far away
The sirens are so very loud
It's then I start to pray

Fighting you
Fighting me
Fighting things
We cannot see

Then the light begins to fade
And so does all the noise
How sad that all this came to be
The life that love destroys

Loving

You're the moon, to my sea
You help me ebb and flow
I move toward your gravity
Bask in your moonlit glow
You're the earth
You're the sky
You're the air that floats on by
Without you
There's no me
Then I'd be a stagnant sea
You're the sun, to my land
You help me grow and grow
I love the way my world's less bland
My sunshine, rain and snow
You're the earth
You're the sky
You're the air that floats on by
Without you
There's no me
And I love that we are we

Waterfall

You sparkle in the sunlight
You smell like morning dew
Your smile to the horizon
I'm so in love with you

Your skin like brand new velvet
So wonderful to view
A tree so full of blossom
Can't take my eyes off of you

Your sense of care so wonderful
You shine like rivers blue
Your heart is warmer than the sun:
I feel at peace with you

It's like I've found a waterfall
White water so see-through
It's perfect fall surrounding me
It's heaven here with you

So cold

I look across the cotton land
Its icy cloak my only view
This bed so cold and very bare
It's nothing without you

I place my arm out at the space
Run fingers where you'd lay
My senses want to feel you
But nothing, just dismay

You

You came to touch
You came to stay
You even took my breath away

You spoke of love
You seemed so kind
You danced inside my troubled mind

You held me tight
You wiped my tears
You even helped me with my fears

You spoke of us
You spoke of care
You spoke of all the things we'd share

You changed one day
You seemed so blind
You lost your way within my mind

You took your things
You went away
You didn't think of me that day

You need to look
You need to find
You need to look inside your mind

You thought of you
You spoke of you
You only thought of what you'd do

Dead end

When love goes down a one-way street
It has nowhere to go
It tries to climb above the wall
So little does it know
For love is wrought without control
It cannot see an end
When alleyways are all it sees
It thinks its heart will mend
Be careful of those giant walls
Take care of whom you love
As one-way streets bring misery
When love can't climb above

Search

I'd climb a hundred mountains
Walk two times round the Earth
I'd even swim the seven seas
To find out what I'm worth

I'd hold my breath for one whole day
Whilst orbiting the moon
I'd sort out global warming
To feel that something soon

I'd even die a death a thousand times
Then rise a thousand more
I'd feed the starving round the world
To find that something more

For I am just unlovable
I struggle with these things
Pleasure, happiness and love
As depression pulls my strings

Hour-long seconds

I hold on for a smile, that tender sign of care
It's then I catch a glimpse of me, reflecting in your eyes
Pausing whilst I look at you, I try hard not to stare
I grasp for air inside my lungs, my heartbeat reaching highs
The long-lost treasure in my life, I hope you realise

Just for a little while

I see her in the crowded bar
She's the parting of the sea
In a blood-red dress without a bra
She turns to look at me

Transfixed, obsessed, I look at her
Just then that perfect smile
I wish that I could capture time
Just for a little while
Just for a little while

Beautiful

It's not what you see
But more what you feel
That sense of enrapture
Your heart there to steal

It will draw your attention
Then capture your gaze
You stare with contentment
Your feelings amaze

Your heart seems to stutter
Your muscles seem weak
That warm inner glow
That pleasure you seek

Such beautiful things
You shouldn't ignore
Your mind needs that pleasure
It needs to adore

Moments

The monster from the sea

I was ten years old and all alone
Awoken from my dream
and cast into the sea

My mother walked away
Despite the scream from me

Just then, a rage from far below
An eye so blank and cold
Staring at me menacingly

Leering at my naked torso
He so adored my agony

Naked strike marks everywhere
My body tossed and torn
Alone inside my misery

But mother loves her monster
She loves him more than me

Cavity

Trapped inside his shadow
The devil makes no sound
His mouth so full of agony
He fights from underground

Gravity
Depravity
Blasphemy
The cavity

Casting shadows from on high
The Gods that make no sound
With mouths so full of harmony
Dispelling underground

Gravity
Depravity
Blasphemy
The cavity

I live my life betwixt the two
Though I can make a sound
My mouth so full of questioning
Religions, things dumbfound

PlayStation

I've marched inside old footsteps
The dust of soldiers past
So strange to walk the same old sands
The fate of lower-classed

I've been to countries far away
To places you've not seen
The times you wondered what to wear
I witnessed things obscene

I've suffered hardships not for you
I'm not sure that you'd care
Your views are snippets on the news
You watch from your armchair

I've often thought about your thoughts
I'm puzzled as to why
For I have seen the worst of man
Yet hear your heavy sigh

I've come to understand one thing
Our lives are not the same
Yours is just expectancy
Mine was not a game

Checkmate

The black queen
Takes the knight
He didn't see her there
The pawns are now all scurrying
The king can only stare

The black queen
Moves to check
Her movement one of stealth
Panic hits the checkered board
The king has lost his wealth

The black queen
Hits the king
Yet still she was not seen
The enemy now broken up
A gunship is the queen

Slaughter

I'm looking back at history, a sum of endless pain
Fractured times of happiness, like slaves tied to a chain
It's money that enraptures us, the rich will always reign
Wars of greed and energy, to feed our need to gain
The rich will always kill the poor, a poor v poor campaign
So many lies within the truth, those lies control the cane
I'm growing tired of the rich, who preach like I'm a stain
I may be poor in money terms; I'm rich inside my brain
But I can't change the way things are, just watch the rich complain
I'm locked up in the cattle truck, aboard the rich man's train

Devil's child

I bumped into the Devil's child
She made me stop and see
Her fiery tongue toward my ear
And then she said to me

See the world ending
There's no chance of mending
Soon you'll be with me
Mankind's not defending
Heavens closed for thee

She referenced inward thinking
History repeating
Of those in power controlling
And of demons tweeting

See the world ending
There's no chance of mending
Soon you'll be with me
Mankind's no defending
Heavens closed for we

Coastal path

A sun-beaten pathway lays under my feet
Cracked and worn by many souls
The journeys of people along the cliff edge
Over bumps, divots and even old holes

The low hugging gorse bush that borders my route
With flowers speckled bright yellow
Small clumps of grass cling to the edge of the cliff
The rusted rocks like sculptures below

The shriek of a seagull breaks me from my thought
Its majesty of thermal flight
The sea comes into view with shimmers of sun
Waves hit the cliff where land and sea fight

The pathway winding whilst descending and climbing
I plod along with utmost care
Stopping here, and stopping there, to admire things
I breathe in the fresh, clean ocean air

The noise of the waves mixed with sounds of a gull
Sea breeze gently fans my skin
Yet I'm alone, surrounded by nature's warmth
In the distance the old smuggler's Inn

Coffin

You walk up to the coffin
Half-opened, just for you
Inside you see the body:
It's someone you once knew

You stand and stare in silence
The body now at rest
Then smell a sweet aroma
See hands wrapped on the chest

That view of death romantic
You think of days gone by
You try to speak but don't know how
(It's then you start to cry)

But death's not always easy
Not when it's seen in war
To hear the screams of agony
The smell like none before

To witness life becoming death
To see souls letting go
The eyes that scan so vividly
Then disappear like snow

To have that person next to you
Zipped up inside a bag
Nothing resplendent in that death
No coffin with a flag

Death involving violence
Will bring you to your knees
To view that body in a box
Won't change those memories

Surf

An unpredictable power
That's clear for you to see
Don't trust the way it talks to you
You mustn't trust the sea

The waves roll in like soldiers
They march in staggered rows
They tumble turquoise into white
Then growl as anger grows

You have to learn your limit
Then whisper softest words
Be on your guard whilst in its grasp
And soar along like birds

So take your board of poly
Then set it on the sea
Caress the water where you are
Then let your spirit free

That board is like a wild steed -
You have to take control
Your feet are your authority
The journey from your soul

So ride your wave with fervour
Embrace the mighty sea
But keep a watch below your board
As the sea might disagree

Birds

The blackbirds like the evergreens
The sparrows love a hedge
The pigeons, they like everywhere
But love a window ledge

The seagulls like to be at sea
The swans beside a lake
Parrots love a mass of trees
But they all enjoy daybreak

Penguins swim in deepest seas
The albatross soars high
Magpies like all shiny things
The cuckoo likes to pry

The peacock has a mighty tail
The coal tit won't eat coal
The robin has the reddest chest
Whilst Eagles will patrol

So many birds around the world
With wingspans great and small
Not all can swim, not all can fly
Yet splendid aren't they all

Free

I lay in grass 6 inches long
The scent like something new
All around me quietness
Small clouds amongst the blue
I hear a birdsong far away
Its melodic rhythm calm
I run my hands amongst the grass
Such softness on my palm
Then a bumble noise nearby
Yet no sign of the bee
I feel like I am part of life
At one with land and sea
Could I be sinking into earth
Or the earth entrenching me
On a day like this, I feel so blessed
A moment to feel free

Angel

Was I born to be an Angel?
I know that sounds so wrong
I've tried so hard to do my work
I've struggled to be strong

I know you think I've lost my mind
Perhaps that might be true
I've tried to see the good in man
I've done my best for you

From childhood to fifty years
I've sought to stop the bad
I soaked up years of nastiness
But now I'm just too sad

I need some time to rest my head
To think through days gone by
The memories are hurting me
Does this mean Angels cry?

Our Father

Our Father
Who art in heaven
Whatever be your name
I'm trying hard to work this out
Why mankind plays your game

They're tempting you in
Receive the Lord
You lovers of hope

Your Brother
Who art in Hell
Whatever be his name
It's torturous to see his work
He's equally to blame

They're tempting you in
Receive the Lord
You lovers of hope

Murderers kneel
Inside your church
To pray and sing your songs
That's all they need to do for you
To rid them of their wrongs

They're tempting you in
Receive the Lord
You lovers of hope

Mine is the kingdom
No power, nor glory
No story to be told

You might suggest my only sin
Not paying you in gold

No tempting me in
Won't meet the Lord
I don't have the hope

Frightened

She peers behind the open door
The sound continues as before
She's staring down the corridor
But nothing there to see

It's then that it gets very cold
The stifling air seems very old
A smell that seems to be like mould
Still nothing there to see

She takes a footstep on the floor
It's something that she can't ignore
The cold, crisp air is very sore
What is it she can't see?

It's then she hears a sudden sound
She's not sure where, she turns around
She feels her heartbeat start to pound
And now she wants to flee

But now she's feeling trapped in time
A part of someone's else's crime
But here's the twist within this rhyme
She's in jail for burglary

My Castle

Atop a carpet made of sand
I stare across the beach
My castle sits in front of me
Beyond the tidal reach

My feet are hidden out of view
My hands are feeling dry
The noise of fun is everywhere
Some children running by

The strength of sun upon my face
The gentle breeze that cools
But lotion needed everywhere
Just see the sunburnt fools

Can't find my bucket nor my spade
As the moon comes into view
I fear the tide is coming in
What will my castle do?

How many castles must we make
They always wash away
My castles used to be ornate
But now they fade to grey

Storm

I stare out of my window
My chin rests on my hand
My eyes are looking at the sky
My thoughts just seem unplanned

The birds are flying all about
No logic to their flight
I see them flying back and forth
But then there's none in sight

The sky once blue is darkening
The air seems very still
I feel my mood is getting low
My eyes drop to the sill

Then the flash across my brow
The rain strikes windowpane
The noise of thunder sounding near
My world lights up again

Strangely I feel safe in here
I watch the storm roll by
Something strangely comforting
It's natures lullaby

The Lurking

I see those shapes so fleetingly
They like to dart around
They like to move behind me
They do not make a sound

They are not tall, nor are they small
They hang around with me
I often see them in the hall
They move mischievously

No blacker thing you'll ever see
Like eclipsing of the sun
They have such fun in taunting me
They often stare, then run

I guess you think I might be mad
Perhaps that might be true
But keep an eye out when you're sad
As they might just play with you

Looking Glass

I have a little looking glass
It helps my eye to see
The things that seem so far away
No longer so for me

I have a little looking glass
It helps my eye to see
Why don't you come and have a look
A look through it with me

I have a little looking glass
It helps my eye to see
So when the days are darkening
I'll find a path for me

I have a little looking glass
It helps my eye to see
I often catch a glimpse of us
Below the willow tree

The Wizard

I need to see the Wizard
I want to see him soon
I'd like for him to put me right
Perhaps one afternoon

The problems not my body
The problems not my heart
The problems deep inside my brain
It's fallen all apart

So if you see a tin man
Perhaps a Scarecrow too
Please tell them of the Lion
And what he needs to do

Painting

At the bottom of the painting
A grass of sun-drenched green
With borders made of poplar trees
Their sway is quite serene
Slightly right of centre
A lady swathed in white
Her elegant umbrella
And corset tied up tight
Beyond a deer magnificent
He's captured in her gaze
Standing proud and wonderful
Amidst the golden maize
The middle fades from gold to white
A gate stands all alone
The season just so summery
The maize remains unsown
Above them all the bluest sky
With a hazy midday sun
The faintest cloud is passing by
My mental painting fun

Soul

A weaker man lives in my soul
Tired, broken and withered,
Tossed and torn
Riddled with invisible carnage
Sobbing like a new born child
Dying an agonising and lonely death
Pausing
Awaiting the calm, translucent sea
Embracing the loss of sound
A noiseless and thoughtless energy
Calmly and beautifully floating skyward
Forgetting everything in the briefest of moments
Smiling that one last time
Turning away from all it has seen, heard, done
No need for need forevermore
No need for anything
Anymore
My now beautiful soul

King with no kingdom

You sit atop your hand-built throne
Of diamond-clustered gold
Draped in so much reverie
Your palace made to scold

A lonely king without a Queen
Your loyal subjects few
Obsessed with poor behaviour
Of course you'd never do

No single heartbeat for the world
No sense of what is true
You're just too blind to see it all
A single-minded view

So whilst your world is standing still
Your throne won't reach the sky
The scorn you thread now wearing thin
Your life is but a lie

Compute

Device not ready
File not found
Access denied
Programme unsound

Bad command
Syntax error
Low disc space
Doesn't seem clever

Out of memory
System fail
Frozen screen
Cannot check mail

Reboot the system
Blue screen shows
I've got a problem
Need to close

Penrose Wood

It's May, a beautiful day
A day to stroll in Penrose wood
I stop to make a memory
Recording where I'm stood

The wooded air upon my skin
Fresh, clean and with hints of sea
The warmth of early summer
Natures quilt surrounding me

Lush green grasses all around
Sunlight flickers pass the trees
The flowers soaking up the sun
Bluebells ring whilst in the breeze

I have spent so many days in here
But the splendour always new
Perhaps I should suggest you come
But I like it without you

Platform 2

I'm sitting on the platform
Its age so very old
White paint defines the platform edge
The stand back line of gold

I look below the platform edge
I see the red brick wall
The grey rocks gather like a sea
I feel I'm ten feet tall

The rusty track with polished top
Sleepers black and browned
The rows of bolts all standing proud
They tie us to the ground

So many trains have come along
A lot of people too
This platform sits here patiently
A Launchpad just for you

Summer 1943

The family walk along the street
Their treasures packed in bags
The little ones are crying out
They walk past reddened flags

All along that weary route
The people stop and stare
Most don't know what's going on
Yet some are well aware

Then they reach the rail yard
They're herded on a train
Screaming comes from carriages
None are seen again

Treasure

There's more to a person than material pleasure
Inside that person lays the greatest of treasure

All that we see

A half-life of wandering through our existence
Unending questions of who or what we are
The preciousness of life we hold so dear
The very things we do usually conflict with others
An overwhelming sense of selfishness
We convince ourselves that we are righteous
That we are the one person who never ever lies
The sole survivor from the Garden of Eden
For everywhere temptation from people
We strive to address all of our fears
Tackling all that is seen as wrong
Frustration hits at every other turn
Trying to be extraordinarily ordinary
Listening to broken words written in hapless code
Watching things people want us to see
Longing for unending and harmonious joy
Striving to set the correct example
Wanting to be liked and loved by all
Searching for what happens after life
Embracing and holding onto hope blindly
Running toward any beacon that offers sanctuary
Racing headlong into confusing situations
Trying so very hard to analyse in the briefest of time
Learning how not to repeat the illness of early days
Memorising memories of things that make no sense
Ruminating in endless circles of despair
Desperately looking for your answer as to why
Trying not to mourn the agonies of our past
Learning each and every minute of every hour
Then drifting into sleep to allow ourselves to rest
Yet mourning sleep upon our awakening

So this is life or is it merely the life of our mind
Take care not to overload your fragile brain

Find time each day for only yourself
Be kind to your thoughts and dreams
Embrace the things that give you peace
Let yourself drift into a parallel universe
Admire and astonish at all you've done
Love everything that you possibly can
Open your heart to all that you feel
Then all that you are will be all that we see

Willow Tree

Willow, Willow, Willow Tree
We're very similar
You and me

Whilst others climb up to the sky
We stay quite low
And wonder why

We twist, we turn, we look so strong
But deep inside
There's something wrong

We weep, we weep, we weep all day
We try so hard
To run away

But we're both rooted to this land
And so I'll stay
To hold your hand

Our arms outstretched and hanging low
We look so sad
Quite rightly so

But Willow Tree I have your back
So we can stop
The lumberjack

Author Biography

As a newcomer to poetry and writing Karl has made quite an impact with his succinct and thought-provoking style. Encouraged by Emma Willis MBE after he'd sent her a thank you poem, Karl's work has been coveted by many. His work has included appearances at festivals and readings around the country. He is hugely passionate about encouraging other sufferers of mental issues to look toward the Arts as a means of therapy.

He took part in the first Mayfair and St. James's Literary Festival launched in November 2018, during which Karl performed his poem 'War not War', alongside Alicia Vikander and Felicity Kendall, as part of the Josephine Hart Poetry Hour - Poetry of the Great War in St. James's Church London, as well as being invited to read this powerful, short work on BBC Radio 3 during Remembrance week.

BBC and Channel 4 News both covered Karl's work shown at the 'Art in the Aftermath' exhibition in Pall Mall, London, featuring a wall covered in hundreds of his poems titled 'The Writings on the Wall'. Response to his work and requests for a book were so overwhelming that he has decided to publish 'Second Life', an insight into the healing power of poetry produced with such urgency by this extraordinary man. Karl writes a poem almost every day and has written over 700 since he came to words as his healing.

You can catch up with Karl by any of the following:

karltearney@gmail.com Email
@karltearney Facebook
@karltearney Instagram
@karltearney Twitter
www.willowtreesociety.co.uk Webpage

About Fly on the Wall Press:

A publisher with a conscience.
Publishing high quality anthologies on pressing issues, chapbooks
and poetry products, from exceptional poets around the globe.
Founded in 2018 by founding editor, Isabelle Kenyon.

Other publications:

Please Hear What I'm Not Saying
(February 2018. Anthology, profit to Mind.)

Persona Non Grata
(October 2018. Anthology, profit to Shelter and Crisis Aid UK.)

Bad Mommy/Stay Mommy by Elisabeth Horan
(May 2019. Chapbook.)

The Woman With An Owl Tattoo by Anne Walsh Donnelly
(May 2019. Chapbook.)

the sea refuses no river by Bethany Rivers
(June 2019. Chapbook.)

Social Media:

@fly_press (Twitter)
@flyonthewall_poetry (Instagram)
@flyonthewallpoetry (Facebook)
www.flyonthewallpoetry.co.uk

CPSIA information can be obtained
at www.ICGtesting.com
Printed in the USA
LVHW011706160719
624282LV00016B/1126/P